The Kabbalah has long languished in darkness, unknown outside the confines of Jewish Mysticism and the communities who practiced it. But today, the Kabbalah is well-known but often misunderstood.

The story of Kabbalah is as old as Judaism itself, with many of the ideas present in the Hebrew Scriptures interpreted in the canon of Kabbalah. Applying Jewish theological premises and Neo-Platonist cosmology, the Kabbalists created a systematic interpretation of familiar Creation Narrative in the Book of Genesis, which today illuminates and serves Judaism. At the same time, Kabbalistic concepts have entered mainstream consciousness with great interest expressed in mainstream Christianity and even in modern science.

You'll find in these pages a completely different way of approaching the mystery of Divinity, the purpose of humanity in Creation, and how we can, in our small, creaturely way, partner with God toward the final healing of Creation and the return of the Messiah and the dawn of Olam Haba (the World to Come).

Kabbalah for Beginners, an Introduction to Jewish Mysticism, is my personal invitation to you to enter a world of bold exploration and humble introspection that has led, over many centuries, to a unique vision for humanity living in intimate relation to the Creator.

Theo Lalvani.

Kabbalah for Beginners

An Introduction to
Jewish Mysticism

Table of Contents

Introduction

While Jewish Mysticism saw its most fruit-
ful flowering during the Medieval Era and
the 18th Century, its roots are found in the ancient
texts of the Hebrew Scriptures. There is even evi-
dence of a mystical interpretation of the scriptures
as early as the 1st Century CE, especially in the esoteric Sefir ha-Bahir (Book of Brilliance).

Today, Jewish Mysticism has reached beyond
Judaism to find itself the object of fascination for
millions of spiritual seekers from all faith back-
grounds. But distortion often follows popularization, and so, we see Kabbalah Centers springing up
all over the world, including "Christian Qabbalah"
and "Hermetic Kabbalah."

But we're here to talk about Jewish Mysticism,
introducing you to some of the primary texts, concepts, and figures responsible for creating the canon of Kabbalah as we know it today.

Mystical movements within the main religions of the world are often marginalized or disregarded by more traditional expressions and interpretations. This is as true of the Sufis of Islam as it is of the Kabbalists of Judaism. But this notion is rapidly changing, as Jews all over the world have started to rediscover the power of Jewish Mysticism, embodied in the books which form the Kabbalistic canon.

In this book, you'll learn:

- Some of Kabbalah's key historical moments and all events that shaped it.
- Who are some of the pivotal sages of Jewish Mysticism.
- What concepts like Shevirot ha-Kelim, tzimtzum, reshimu and tikkun mean in the Lurianic framework of Kabbalah.
- What the ultimate aim of Kabbalah is.
- The true meaning of "tikkun olam."

Let's whet your appetite for this fascinating subject with an introductory overview of Kabbalah, its spirituality, and how it came to be. I hope you'll find, in these pages, valuable information that supports your own spiritual journey.

Chapter One:

In the Beginning

Traditionalists place the knowledge which would be developed into Kabbalah in the hands of Primordial Man – Adam. In the Kabbalistic understanding, Adam was created with all the knowledge necessary to bring about Creation's perfection.

But there was a hindrance in the creative schema, occasioned by the breaking of vessels in the heavenly realms. These vessels, called kelipot, contained the Ohr Ein Sof – the Light of the Limitless - but they were unequal to the task and shattered from the intense pressure of this Divine Light. Referred to as the Shevirot ha-kelim (the Breaking of the Vessels), this event brings forth the explanation for the existence of evil in Creation.

I suppose you could call it a "technical problem," while the kelipot seemed like a good idea at the time, containing the Light of the Limitless (Ein Sof or God) in clay vessels didn't exactly pan out.

Later, we'll find out how these fractured vessels were transformed to become the sefirot.

The Kabbalistic interpretation of Creation is a complex system that requires the understanding of the "why" and the "how" behind the Created Order. For centuries, sages have poured over existing Kabbalah scriptures and traditions and have created their own commentaries and examinations, all dedicated to the project of understanding why God created the universe as we know it and what humanity's role is in that Created Order.

The word "Kabbalah" means "reception," referring specifically to the esoteric knowledge of the Hebrew Scriptures, revealed through lifelong study, contemplation, and meditation. With the first recipient of this knowledge identified as Adam, Moses, Judaism's most preeminent Prophet, was said to have later received it at Mt. Sinai in the form of Oral Torah. Simultaneously, tradition states that Moses received the written Torah in its entirety.

Early Jewish Mysticism

Oral Torah stands in Jewish Mysticism as an authoritative complement to the written Torah (the first 5 books of the Bible – Genesis, Exodus, Leviticus, Numbers, and Deuteronomy). Orthodox Jews consider the liturgical, spiritual, and legal aspects of this book to be of primary importance to their spiritual practice. The 613 mitzvot (commandments which, when kept, are believed to bring the Created Order to its perfected state) are derived from the Oral Torah. The mitzvot cover everything from how Jews are to worship to the practice of kashrut (orthodoxy in consuming food) to how people are to dress to model fidelity to God.

Only following the destruction of the Second Temple in 70 CE did the codification (transcription and compilation in book form) of the Oral Torah begin to occur. Before that time, Oral Torah was transmitted from mouth to ear, generation to generation. With the destruction of the center of Jewish religious life, the Jews were dispersed. With the Temple in Jerusalem destroyed for the second time, Jews sought to canonize the Oral Torah, creating a series of key manuscripts as they did so.

The Mishnah and the Gemara (commentaries and discussions about the Mishnah) form the Talmud, which contains the laws of the Oral Torah.

However, the Talmud was created in two versions. The first was produced in Galilee, Israel, from 300 – 250 CE and is known as the Jerusalem Torah. The second is the more thorough treatment of the subject matter, produced between 450 and 500 CE and known as the Babylonian Talmud, having been produced during the Jewish Exile in Babylon.

In about the 5th Century, a school of Jewish Mysticism, Merkavah Mysticism, arose during the editing of the Tanakh (the complete written Torah). This mystical impulse in Judaism was referred to as both Ma'aseh Merkavah and Ma'aseh Bereshit. The first phrase means "the work of the Chariot" and the second, "the work of Creation."

The Chariot in question is, of course, that of the Biblical Prophet Ezekiel. The literature produced by Merkavah Mysticism is called "heikhalot" (palaces) literature, and this is most likely the closest we'll ever get to a "ground zero" for the establishment of Kabbalah as a distinct movement within Judaism.

Seeking esoteric knowledge that was not expressly and plainly stated was the aim of Merkavah Mystics, seeking to draw closer to the Divine by employing the messages in the text of Ezekiel's

Divine Chariot (which could be teased out through close examination of the text and approaching the language creatively and spiritually).

Key texts in this early layer of Jewish Mysticism were Ezekiel, chapters 1 and 2, and Isaiah 6. But the whispers of Jewish Mysticism can be read in many other Biblical narratives, particularly in that of Jacob wrestling an Angel (Genesis 32:22 – 32; Hosea 12: 4) and the Jacob's Ladder narrative in Genesis 28.

In the case of Isaiah 6, the text addresses Isaiah's vision of God on his Throne in the Temple, calling Isaiah to his prophetic role, commissioned to convey a dire message to the Israelites. This vision stands as a central text for the Kabbalistic interpretation of humanity's relationship with God, portraying its intimacy and its purpose – which is to restore Creation to its intended perfection.

Rising from this earliest manifestation of Jewish Mysticism, the collection of documents known as the Dead Sea Scrolls found at Qumran, as well as the Book of Daniel, can be typified as emanating from the same Mystic tradition while carrying on the vestiges of the Prophetic tradition after the

Sack of Jerusalem and the destruction of the Second Temple.

Merkavah Mysticism's aim, though, was not only to witness the Throne of God as Ezekiel had. These early mystics were anxious to unpack the Creation Story in a spiritualized but rational way. Here, the Merkavah Mystics found inspiration in the words of Greek philosophers, specifically those of the Neo-Platonist school. At this point, we see the development of Kabbalah as an encounter between Judaism and the many worlds it inhabited in the diaspora (dispersal), leading to its first flowering in the Middle Ages.

The Middle Ages

The study and development of Kabbalah blossomed again in Medieval Europe, beginning in the 12th Century.

But Kabbalah was, at this point, still very much in the closet. Groups of enthusiasts were private and practiced secretly, under the radar, due to the mysticism they espoused. Rising from this informal setting, the establishment of Kabbalah as an actual

movement is sited in the prov
Languedoc in France.

It wasn't until near the end
that Sefer ha-Bahir was compi
of writings collected into a sir   Considered to be the oldest example in the Kabbalistic canon, Sefer ha-Bahir contains the first graphic
representation of the sefirot (which we'll discuss in
the next chapter).

From the south of France, Kabbalah traveled to
northeastern Spain, where the sage Nahmanides
(1194 – 1270) continued in the earlier tradition of
the Merkavah Mystics by advancing a Hellenistic
framework for his interpretations and commentaries concerning Sefer ha-Bahir and the sefirot.

The Spanish Kabbalists, in the late 13th Century, produced what is arguably the best-known book
in the Kabbalistic tradition, the Zohar (the Book of
Splendor). Because of Judaism's steadfast vision of
a God who is not only one, but inviolably so, the
Zohar was chiefly concerned with the tension and
the unity between opposites. This is also rooted in
the integrity of good and evil as a mutually depen-
dent tension.

Medieval Kabbalists, the Zohar was the fullness of Kabbalah. Today, it continues to stand as a pillar of Kabbalistic thought. Its publication is the locus classicus of Jewish Mysticism and the foundation of the Kabbalistic framework of Isaac Luria (1534 – 1572), considered to be the chief architect of Kabbalistic thought.

The Spanish Expulsion – 1492

Jewish History is punctuated by times of extreme persecution, sometimes going on for centuries and stretching across entire continents. Following the Babylonian Exile and the subsequent destruction of the Second Temple by the Romans, the Jews were dispersed throughout Europe. Subsequently, Spain became one of the most productive centers of Medieval Kabbalistic study and thought.

But the Spanish Expulsion of 1492 was to change everything. This event was the culmination of the sustained persecution of Jews in Europe, particularly by the Crusades (1095 – 1271), which rolled through the continent, destroying entire communities and displacing survivors.

This brutal setting was to turn the Jews of Europe inward, seeking the comfort of Messianic hope in an enhanced spirituality. Part of that quest was the land of Israel, with European Jews seeking shelter from the storm of anti-Semitism in Europe.

Fleeing Europe, Jews returned to their historical homeland, creating a bubbling stew of Jewish tradition and thought, including Jewish Mysticism, in the city of Safed. From this stew emerged Moses Cordovero (1522 – 1570), who was largely responsible for refocusing Kabbalah on the hope of a coming Messiah. After exile in Babylon and the destruction of Rome, Jews were once again exiled and seeking succor. Cordovero's work, which encompassed the popularization of the Zohar, led to a renaissance in Judaism, centered in the Holy Land.

Born in Safed, Isaac Luria was to take up Cordovero's mantle after arriving in Safed in 1569. Today, he is known as the ARI or Arizal (the Lion).

At only 22 years of age, Isaac Luria began his intense study of Kabbalah, eventually becoming a respected sage and teacher. It was Luria's tremendous influence, which continues to this day, that led to Jewish Mysticism rising to the challenge of mending the brokenness of the people in exile.

Luria built on Cordovero's Messianic focus, adding to it the recurring theme of exile, so lamentably familiar to the community at Safed. But Luria didn't do a great deal of writing. Instead, he relied on person-to-person transmission among his students. But even without a written record, Luria's insights were to form the basis of Kabbalah, and by the middle of the 17th Century, Isaac Luria's ideas were known to most Jews across Europe.

Of all Luria's students, Chaim Vital (1542 – 1620) was the most prolific, collecting transcriptions of the sage's lessons. From these transcriptions, Vital was to produce the 8 volumes of Etz Chaim (the Tree of Life), derived from the Zohar and Luria's teachings on it. These 8 volumes were to become the basis of what we know as Lurianic Kabbalah.

Etz Chaim and Kitvei Ari

Because of the esoteric nature of Kabbalistic writings, much of what was found in them prior to the work of Isaac Luria through his student, Chaim

Vital, was impenetrable. This changed with the publication of the Etz Chaim, which served to illuminate the Zohar, offering prayers for daily life, specific Festivals, and other occasions and for the Sabbath.

Chaim Vital would also transcribe all Luria's lessons in a collection of books known as "Kitvei Ari" (the Writings of the Lion). So, while Isaac Luria didn't write much down, Chaim Vital saw the value in doing so. Because of his work, the Lurianic Kabbalah became the basis of the canon of Kabbalah, in the form of the Kitvei Ari. These served to shed light on the mysteries of previous writings like the Zohar and Sefer ha-Bahir, as well as the famed Sefer Yetzirah (the Book of Formation).

While Isaac Luria only lived to be 38 years old, he is indisputably one of the chief influences to shape Kabbalah as we know it today. His work is the basis for the rising of Chassidim in Ukraine. From there, Kabbalah grew to be disseminated and studied all over the world, tumbling over inter-religious boundaries.

Chapter Two:

The Aleph Bet of Creation

Isaac Luria said that Kabbalah is the inner soul of the Torah. And at the heart of that assertion is the Hebrew language itself. Long lost in all but its religious application in prayers and holy books, Hebrew floated in a limbo between death and life for thousands of years.

But the sages and scribes have always understood the mystical element of the Hebrew language, most fulsomely expressed in its written form. In its written form, there is an elegance and power which lend themselves to the contemplation of the individual letters. While this book is too narrow in scope to discuss the work of Abraham Abulafia (1240 – circa 1291), it was Abulafia who would develop a science of language rooted in his explorations of Hebrew that led to Natural Language Processing (NLP) in Artificial Intelligence.

Abulafia believed that by randomly combining Hebrew characters and esoteric interpretations, secret coded messages could be extrapolated from Hebrew Scripture. And in Kabbalah, the characters of the Hebrew language have a special and unusual role.

The letters form Creation itself. It is through their agency that Creation was facilitated, with each character performing a specific role, according to Sefer Yetzirah (the Book of Formation). And it was from this Kabbalistic work that Abulafia drew his inspiration for his science of language.

Appearing to be random on the surface, Abulafia based his methodology on the book's descriptions of Creation coming about via the combination of various Hebrew characters. Going further, Abulafia posited that the symbols represented by the characters themselves were transformational, offering unknown ways into scripture through the application of Sefer Yetzirah's formulae and contemplations.

Linguistic Mysticism – "What Cannot Be Said."

Just as the Holy Name of God may not be pronounced in Judaism, there is a philosophical concept that there are also ideas that may be not be expressed as speech. While the idea of the creative power of the Hebrew Aleph Bet is central to Kabbalistic thought, running alongside that creative power is the belief that some words and letters are unpronounceable.

And so, the reconciliation of the tension between the creative agency of letters and their unspeakableness is found in the holiness ascribed to what they represent – in their symbolic written nature.

The letter Aleph is the first letter of the Hebrew aleph bet (the alphabet in English, as we take the Greek name). In Jewish Mysticism, Aleph holds an elevated and esoteric place, as it is considered unpronounceable and the spiritual source of all the other letters after it in the aleph bet. Due to that status, Aleph stands as the condition by which the Hebrew language exists – the first principle.

The letter Aleph reflects the ineffability of the Divine – unknowable, transcendent, and yet, immanent in the Created Order. (Again, note the tension between transcendence – God above and beyond and immanence – God infused into all that is).

Like traditional Rabbinical Judaism, Jewish Mysticism holds to the tension between opposites as a defining principle of the Created Order. In this, the treatment of the letter Aleph is both sacred (set apart) and profane (mundane), is consistent.

One of the most illustrative examples of the tension between opposites is that of the existence of good and evil. Whether evil exists in the Created Order as the result of an error provoking a cataclysm (Shevirot ha-Kelim) or as the carefully calculated action of God thrown into the mix as an invitation to the exercise of free will, is irrelevant. Both conceptualizations of reality are valid, as, without evil, we would not have the ability to discern goodness.

According to Rabbinical Judaism, an explanation is found in the Midrash, in Genesis Rabbah 9:7. It explains that without yetzer ha-ra (the urge to do evil), ambition would not exist. If the only urge extent in human nature was the yetzer ha-tov (the urge to do good), we'd all stop working, having children, and striving for better lives. The commentary itself seeks to reconcile the existence of evil, referencing Genesis 1:31, in Torah, which reads, "God saw everything that he had made and indeed, it was very good." The yetzer ha-ra offers us free will, which all human life is gifted as part of the bargain. Without the existence of evil, what choice is there to make?

And so, in the letter Aleph, we see our first clue about the theological underpinnings of Judaism and Jewish Mysticism both, which is the tension between opposites, as posited by Heraclitus (c. 535 – c. 475 BCE), one of the later philosophers, and Plato's most important influences.

In this respect, Aleph holds a similar status to the Tetragrammaton (YHVH). This is the unpronounceable name of the Creator, due to its holiness and the ineffable reality it describes is preeminent as "what cannot be said." It is. We know it is. So, as we acknowledge it as holy, we bow to its numinous power by keeping it out of our mouths.

However, Aleph is part of the Hebrew language – now a living, public language as well as a religious, liturgical language. The idea of the "set apart" nature of the letter Aleph in the Kabbalistic treatment of language as a spiritual vehicle speaks directly to Jewish Mysticism's stated purpose – humanity's union with God.

Of course, this doesn't exist on our humble, earthy plane in the grand scheme of things. Some of us may find union with God in our ways. That does not imply that we all have. Had we all found our ways to that union, we would have achieved the state of "tikkun" (meaning "repair") – Isaac Luria's concept of the ultimate repair of a Creation corrupted by the Breaking of the Vessels.

While the created human speaks the language of which Aleph is a part of, that part represents the tension between the Divine that we reach toward and the material in which we live. With a God both transcendent and immanent, tongue-tied humanity trips over the Aleph – not yet ready to pronounce the spiritual progenitor of the Hebrew language.

Aleph can thus be shown, spoken, and seen in creaturely human life. But in its esoteric form, it is "what cannot be said." Spiritually set aside, the Aleph is sacred, but it is also, in its created form, a profane agent of communication.

Lashon Hakodesh

Hebrew is often referred to as the "Holy Tongue." Nachmanides (1193 – 1270), also known by the acronym "RAMBAN," said that the Hebrew language is holy because God used it to communicate what was expected of the Israelites through the Prophets.

But probably the greatest single argument for the holiness of the Hebrew language is the Bible itself. While the Tanakh is written primarily in Hebrew, some of its books are written substantially in Aramaic, which the Jews wrote and spoke during the Babylonian Exile.

And because this book is about Kabbalah, the Creation Narrative of the Book of Genesis is Exhibit "A" in any discussion of Hebrew's characterization as the lashon hakodesh.

Kabbalah, in fact, is primarily concerned with a spiritual understanding and penetration of the Creation Narrative, and so the mysticism associated with the Hebrew language in Jewish Mysticism is key to that effort.

Because God "spoke" Creation into being, and that speech was Hebrew.

The 10 Utterances

In the Creation Narrative of Genesis, the phrase "and God said" occurs 10 times in the text of the first chapter of the book, from verse 3 through verse thirty (specifically, Genesis 1:3, 1:6, 1:9, 1:11, 1:14-15, 1:20, 1:26, 1:28, 1:29-30).

The number "10" is hugely significant in the Hebrew Scriptures and in Jewish Mysticism. The number of the Commandments given to Moses on stone tablets was 10, as is the number of sefirot. But in a larger context – that of the human creature – there are 10 fingers on human hands and 10 toes on human feet (generally speaking).

The sefirot themselves are connected to the 10 utterances of the Creation Narrative, each corresponding to an act of Creation (Sefer ha-Bahir). Each representing an attribute of God, the sefirot perform as emissaries of the Divine, speaking to us on behalf of God and bearing, in their interconnected, interactive world, the Divine Will.

Beyond the number of utterances, though, is the idea that the Divine Will, arising in the "mind" of God as an "idea" – a spark of inspiration – became infused into the Created Order through the power of speech. That speech, propelled by the same breath that was breathed into the mud doll that was the Creation of Adam (Gen. 2:7), was the Creative agent employed by the Creator of all that is. Why, when this action might have been taken with telepathy or even a simple gesture? We're talking about an omnipotent Creator, so why speech?

Perhaps, the reason is in the infusion of the Divine Will in the Created Order. As "the Word of our God shall stand forever" (Isaiah 40:8). By uttering Creation into existence, the immanency of God stands forever in every fiber of all that has been created. Stamped with the Divine Will, Creation is forever indelibly marked by its essential nature, which is a material expression of God's deepest desire.

This lofty conception of language as the Divine Architect's most active tool elevates the lashon ha-kodesh to the status of a co-creative force, issuing from the mind of God as the same breath that animated the newly created mud doll.

In the Kabbalistic conception of a Creation spoken into being, the removal of the letters of the "Word of God" would result in a nullified Creation.

Like the heart beating inside a human body, the "Word of God" which animates the Created Order once removed, would result in the reversion of that Order to the state it was prior to God's 10 utterances – that of the "formless void" (Gen. 1:2).

So, when Abraham Abulafia developed his science of language, he wasn't playing around with letters. He wasn't performing a trick with smoke and mirrors. Abulafia was entering into the Divine mystery of a Creation spoken into being, the "Word of God" infusing every cell and particle of it. He was seeking the mystery of Creation in its most visible manifestation of the "Word of God" – the lashon hakodesh.

While the subject of linguistic mysticism in Judaism and Jewish Mysticism is far too complex and vast to cover fully in the simple introduction to Kabbalah offered in this book, I strongly counsel readers to pursue it, as it greatly illuminates the study and understanding of Kabbalah.

In our next chapter, we'll find out about the sefirot, what they mean and how they fit into the great scheme of Kabbalistic thinking.

Chapter Three:

Etz Chaim – The Tree of Life

The sefirot first appear in Kabbalah in Sefer ha-Bahir and Sefer Yetzirah. With the "ruach" (Divine breath) that spoke Creation into being via the 10 utterances standing as the first creative emanation (expelled by creative inspiration), the 10 sefirot correspond to the 10 utterances, maintaining immanence beyond what had already been infused into the Created Order.

These 10 Divine "emissaries" create a means by which humanity can "know" God (the ineffable) through emanations representing God's most compelling traits. Let's meet them.

- Keter (Crown)
- Chokhmah (Wisdom)
- Binah (Understanding)
- Chesed (Lovingkindness)
- Gevurah (Might)

- Tiferet (Beauty)

- Hod (Splendor)

- Netzah (Victory)

- Yesod (Foundation)

- Shekhinah (Divine Presence) is also referred to as Malkhut (Sovereignty). NB: Shekhinah is a unique emanation, sitting at the base of the Tree as its roots and representing the reality of an immanent God who is "with us" (Deuteronomy 31:6, Isaiah 41:10).

These 10 emanations are organized into the Tree of Life (Etz Chaim), echoing the "inner soul" of Torah and the Tree of Life, itself, standing in the Garden of Eden (Gen. 2:9). Arranged in this manner, the sefirot exist both as themselves, independent of the others, and in creative, dynamic interchange, with each sefirah containing the others, simultaneously.

The Etz Chaim schema of the Tree of Life represents a microcosm of the idea of "panentheism" – that all is in God (as opposed to God being in all things), pointing to a holistic relationship between God and Creation. There is no division between the

Divine and the Created Order, just as there is no division between the sefirot. An example of this is the idea that might (Gevurah) accompanies beauty (Tiferet), with each existing not only within the Tree but within and for each other.

A Balanced Creation

The tension at the heart of the Created Order holds all things together, and this reality is fundamental to Etz Chaim as an organizing model for the operation of God's attributes in that Order.

The Tree is arranged according to the energetic nature of the sefirot, with traits of God's unstinting goodness and grace in the "pillar" of the tree on the right, namely Chokhmah (wisdom), Chesed (lovingkindness), and Netzach (victory). These "friendly" attributes are balanced by those on the left side, which speak of God's judgment, namely Binah (understanding), Gevurah (might), and Hod (splendor).

The attributes located on the right –also referred to as the "Pillar of Mercy" mitigate the attributes on the left. Balance and tension, then, are baked into

Etz Chaim to echo the balance and tension in the Created Order.

At the top of the Tree, in the central Pillar, stands Keter (crown). Specifically, this is the Crown of the Most High.

At the bottom of Etz Chaim is Yesod (foundation), the stabilizing roots of the structure extending into the earth, in which we find Shekhinah/Malkhut (Divine Presence). Standing apart from the 10 sefirot of the Tree of Life, the Divine Presence is how humanity and the Creation in which they have been placed in may experience the fullness of God. Nourishing Etz Chaim, Shekhinah is also the principle from which the sefirot operate – the immanence of the Divine in the Created Order.

Running down the center of the Tree, we first find the attribute Tiferet (beauty) uniting the two sides of the tree. This sefirah represents a synthesis of Chesed on the right and Gevurah on the left, processing the two into the balanced, steady, and unchanging nature of the Divine- with justice and mercy both being necessary for the universe to operate as it was intended to.

So, the sefirot not only tell us what God's attributes are, they speak to us of how judgment functions in Creation – as being mitigated by mercy. They reveal to us the true nature of a Divine Creator as an entity with a steady hand and the endless wisdom to dispense measured judgment, tempered by boundless mercy. But that boundless mercy is also mitigated by the presence of judgment, neither dominating nor weak, both informing the other.

The Union of the Sacred and the Profane

Here, I will take French sociologist Emile Durkheim's (1858 – 1917) construct of the sacred and profane as our starting point.

While we tend to think of these two words as being equivalent to "good" (sacred) and "evil" (profane), Durkheim saw that division as arbitrary and rooted in a materialist dualism. In truth, those realities deemed sacred may represent what either good or evil or a combination of the two (which most things, including human beings, are) is. And the profane is merely the mundane – not unlike the letter "Aleph" as both a material agent of communication and the sacred, unpronounceable progenitor of all other Hebrew characters. Aleph is both things, simultaneously and in tension.

The Tree of Life is a balanced embodiment that encompasses both the friendly and the fearsome attributes of an unknowable (yet approachable) God that stands as a model for human activity on earth. This is especially crucial in Judaism, as Jews are called to bring about the final reconciliation between humanity and the Creator, ushering in the Eschaton – the final things in which heaven and earth are united to reflect the original Divine Will in the creative act.

The Song of Moses, given to the people, points to the ultimate unification of heaven and earth and the requirement to two witnesses to be present in legal proceedings under Jewish Law. But within Moses' invocation of the two is a clue about what humanity is here to do.

"Give ear, O heavens, and I will speak; let the earth hear the words of my mouth." (Deuteronomy 32: 1).

Here, Moses calls on both the heavenly realms and those of the Created Order. The implication is that, while separate realities, they're in unity. Further, while God is transcendent, God is imminent ("with us") in the Created Order, and the separation between the heavens and the earth is temporary.

That separation is temporary because of the eschatological role of humanity – to bring about reconciliation between God and Creation in the repair of the catastrophic Breaking of the Vessels.

In the balance, tension, and unity of Etz Chaim, humanity is offered an example of how to proceed, putting balance at the forefront to ensure that the realities of heaven and earth draw closer to one another.

In this is the true purpose of Kabbalah – the mastery and perfection of the soul. This may only be achieved, in mystical terms, through actions that seek and advance reconciliation, namely, by meditation, prayer, and the fulfillment of the mitzvot (blessed actions).

The sefirot, standing as the emissaries of God's attributes and a living snapshot of what God is like, provides humanity with a model to emulate. Through the exertions of the pious, humanity sees its potential reflection in the sefirot – an interpretation of what was intended by "let us make humankind in our image, according to our likeness" (Gen. 1:26).

The Limitless - YHVH

But why are these 10 emissaries of God's attributes available to instruct us as to the nature of God, and why is Shekhinah, the Divine Presence, indwelling Creation?

Because what is without limit can neither be named nor known. And the name given to God by the Jewish Mystics is Ein Sof – the Limitless. Creatures have limits. But Ein Sof, limitless and ineffable, is beyond all understanding. Ein Sof is not, for example, the moon or the sun.

The difference between the Creation and its Creator can be discerned in Genesis 1:16, in which the Divine names the moon and sun. Worshipped by Pagans in the historical setting in which Genesis was written, God reduces the presumed power of these heavenly bodies by naming them "lesser light" (the moon) and "greater light" (the sun). Thus named, the planets are reduced to their creatureliness. No longer the objects of worship as they have been named by their Creator; put in their place as objects in the creative project of the One God – the limitless Ein Sof.

Therefore, the Tetragrammaton is unpronounceable. The Limitless will not be subject to naming, for what you may name is circumscribed and has clearly defined boundaries.

This is not applicable to YHVH. Exodus 3: 13 – 15 is the Biblical source of the Tetragrammaton. This is the Burning Bush narrative, in which Moses asks God to reveal the Divine Name. God answers, in verse 14, "I am who I am."

But the Tetragrammaton is the embodiment of the Hebrew verb to be in all its forms: past, present, and future tenses. So, what God means is, "I will be what I will be" and "I have been what I have been," as well as "I am who I am." In other words – "Don't ask!"

The Tetragrammaton expresses the ineffable mystery of the Divine, demanding that history tell the story of the actions of that entity, as God is ever-present in every moment of the Created Order, simultaneously and eternally – without limitation.

And so, Etz Chaim becomes a road map for the soul seeking the truth about the nature of God. By creating a bridge between the human soul and the Limitless, the sefirot teach and illustrate while bearing with them all the knowledge required to "see" God in the attributes they represent but also in the behavior of the sefirot within the Tree itself. Interactive, collaborative, and yet wholly independent from one another, the sefirot model to us the longed-for potential of the human creature.

Placed in the Garden as God's stewards, humanity creates its own catastrophe in the wake of Shevirot ha-Kelim. Disobediently ignoring the prohibition against eating fruit from the Tree of the Knowledge of Good and Evil, Adam falls from grace, compounding the damage (Gen. 3:1 – 7). Placed in the heart of God's expression of exuberant life, humanity blows it.

But the apple is just the tip of the iceberg. In the world of Kabbalah, the story of Creation is a complex universe of behind-the-scenes action. It's a long-term project in which the fallen stewards of Creation are given a second chance to co-create the intended, final form of a united Creation.

Our next chapter will explore the Kabbalistic concept of Creation, according to the ARI – Isaac Luria.

Chapter Four:

Making Space

"In the beginning when God created the heavens and the earth, the earth was a formless void and darkness covered the face of the deep..."
Genesis 1:2a

C an you make something from nothing?

Theologically speaking – and that's the world we're in as we explore Kabbalah – the omnipotent creative force known as God can do anything, so why not?

But this claim has no philosophical support, save faith itself. And so, in interpreting the structure and order of Creation, the Jewish Mystics followed the cosmology of the Ancient Greeks, namely the father of cosmology in that setting, Parmenides (5th BCE).

Parmenides declared "ex nihilo nihil fit" (from nothing, nothing comes), and it was his influence and that of his fellow Greek philosophers that the writers of the Greek translation of the Hebrew Scriptures, the Septuagint, followed.

So, what does the "formless void" that the Creator "moved over" (Gen 1:2b) mean?

While the void may well be formless and dark, it is not immaterial. What the void represents in the Greek conception of the cosmos is the potential to become something. The formless void, then, is the raw material that awaits the organizing hand of a creative force.

In Hebrew, the "formless void" of Genesis 1 is "tohu wa bohu." Found primarily in the Book Isaiah, the expression is interpreted to mean "primordial chaos" – a disordered state which, while material, is without form or purpose.

But the point of the formless void – tohu wa bohu – is that the organizing principle came in the form of a Creator who knew what was required to mold from primordial chaos and ordered Creation, igniting the raw material of the void with the spark of Divine inspiration.

The Exiled God

As we discussed in the previous chapter, God in the Kabbalistic framework is described as Ein Sof – the limitless, also meaning the "essence" of Divinity. But we've also discussed how all that exists in the Created Order is limited by way of its creaturely status.

So, how did a limitless God create what is limited? How did the Divine creative power manage to give birth to such a circumscribed reality from the infinite existence of the ineffable?

God contracted. God hid. God exiled Divinity to the corner. God curled up in a ball and deliberately separated the Divine from the Created Order. In the Kabbalistic construct of Creation, this act in the Creative process is called "tzimtzum" (contraction).

In so doing, Ein Sof limited the Divine potential by making space for Creation. Imagine yourself in a confined space like an elevator. You need to make room for others as the doors open and the elevator fills, so you make yourself smaller. Passing someone on the street, you make space for those coming toward you. This is what Ein Sof did in the tzimtzum – God limited the vastness of Divinity to create space for Creation.

While many of the sages of Kabbalah have applied a gradual interpretation to tzimtzum, Isaac Luria saw this contraction as sudden; a quantum leap that applied limits to the limitless, thus transforming the Divine in the process.

Chaim Vital, Luria's student and, subsequently, his scribe, wrote in his magisterial series, Etz Chaim, that tzimtzum was a simultaneous transformation of Ohr Ein Sof (the Light of the Limitless). As you'd think, Ohr Ein Sof, as the Light of Divinity, is a manifestation of its source. But according to Isaac Luria, the transformative effect of tzimtzum entailed that Ohr Ein Sof take on the characteristics of light in its limited created version.

Ohr Ein Sof, therefore, is hiding in plain sight in Creation, disguised as the created version of the Light of the Limitless. Just as you can't gaze directly at the sun, you can't encounter the Light of Limitless, unfiltered, in the fullness of its infinite power.

The message of tzimtzum is clear –God desired Creation to the extent that limiting Divine power in a strategic retreat was not too great a price to pay. Tzimtzum, then, is an act of both Divine love and a desire so powerful that God was willing to become limited while, at the same time, remaining the eternal, infinite reality God has always been, is now, and always will be (YHVH).

And again, in tzimtzum is the tension that holds together the vast universe in opposites which form part of a harmonious whole.

And just to be sure, we're perfectly clear – God did not change. God transformed. In order to make something of the primordial, formless void, God contracted both away from the Created Order and toward it. But in that contraction, Creation was infused with the power of the Limitless, in every fiber of the finished product and in the emissaries of God's attributes, the sefirot.

Conceived as immutable and integrated, God is also ineffable. This word is important, as it tells us that we may not know the ways of the Divine (Isaiah 55: 8-9, "For my thoughts are not your thoughts," etc.). God will be what God will be/has been/is.

But the transformation inherent in tzimtzum is strategic, intended to disguise and thus shield the Created Order from God's full and terrible glory. "I, God, do not change" (Malachi 3:6) means exactly what it says. While doing what's necessary to bring Creation into being, God also dons a veil and slinks into the darkness. Like the Wizard of Oz, God is behind the curtain, pulling the levers. But unlike the Wizard of Oz, God is so vast and awe-inspiring that accommodations must be made for the weak of heart and for the sake of making space for a Divinely inspired Creation.

And while God is making space for the massive project that is Creation, God is also making space for the free will of humanity.

A conception of the Divine as a string-pulling, prayer-answering parental force, guiding the universe toward the Eschaton may be comforting for some, but the ineffable God is less of an authoritarian in this model of Creation than a gentle teacher, employing a didactic model that demands more of the student's curiosity than the teacher's ability to deposit key information. Instead of demanding conformity to the demands of the Divine, God hides, asking that we strike out in search of the truth about the Creator.

Free will means humanity has a choice – to seek God by following the breadcrumbs dropped on a woodland trail, hiding between the fresh shoots of grass and the drops of rain as they fall to earth – or not. So tzimtzum is more than a contraction. It's an invitation.

Shevirah (Shevirot ha-Kelim)

The breaking of the vessels stands as the Kabbalistic explanation as to why evil exists in the Creation of a just Creator. But in the breaking is the solution.

In the Kabbalistic narrative, the 10 sefirot were originally conceived as simple clay containers, created for the purpose of storing the Ohr Ein Sof. But the clay pots were not equal to the task and shattered.

The Shevirot ha-Kelim was a cosmic cataclysm, setting loose the broken pieces of the clay containers. The result was brokenness becoming part of the Created Order, marring its perfection - the "very good" state in which it was Created and then found pleasing by its Creator.

The shattering of the vessels represents a shattering of a far profound nature. This event, in the mystical interpretation of the Creation Narrative of Genesis, describes the shattering of the ideal realization of Divine inspiration. Both the Light of the Limitless, dispersed and veiled in creaturely light, and the ruined shards of its former confinement disappear into the wilds of Creation, as the Creator regroups, contracted and concealed.

But simultaneously and ineffably, from the shattered pieces of the frail clay vessels, the sefirot become the first step in a long repair process intended to reconcile humanity to its Creator.

While it's true that we creatures had nothing at all to do with the Shevirot ha-Kelim, it's instructive to understand that we, too, are made from clay and just as fragile. In this idea is a truth about the recurring theme of brokenness in the Jewish canon of Holy Scripture.

For a moment, let's consider the 10 Commandments. The first set given to Moses was broken and was carried in the Ark of the Covenant by the wanderers along with the second set that remained whole, after tradition (Talmud Bava Batra 13b).

The brokenness of the first set of command-ments would come to be reconciled by the second, whole set, dwelling together in the Ark of the Cov-enant. But its brokenness reminds the People of the Covenant of what we all bear within us in our bro-ken, human hearts, most fully human in that bro-kenness. On a more esoteric level, it reminds them of the brokenness of humanity's relationship with God.

Reshimu

Reshimu is what remains after the events of tzimt-zum and Shevirot ha-Kelim. Directly translated as "residue," reshimu is also referred to as "the letters of the residue."

Look at any bottle containing cooking oil in your kitchen cupboard, and you'll see a residue, a film that lingers on the sides of the bottle after the oil has been poured. Reshimu is cosmic post-it notes, reminding us that the Divine has voluntarily chosen to limit itself and that Ohr Ein Sof has taken on a creaturely dress. Posing as natural, creaturely light, the presence of Divine Light hides in plain sight, while God lurks in the darkness.

In a manner of speaking, the sefirot may be conceptualized as residue/reshimu of their former realities – that of the clay pots that held the Light of the Limitless – but not quite. In truth, the sefirot are a transformation of the prototype, containing the very traits of the Divine, defining and reaching out as emissaries to humanity. Clearly defined and interacting among us as living realities, they are reshimu plus.

Another way to wrap your head around the idea of reshimu is to think of it as parallel to memory. Our memories bring us much joy, as well as pain. While they're available to us, we are not living in our memories – even in cases of Post-Traumatic Stress Disorder. Our memories come to us from the lives we have already lived and are no longer in the present. They are only available to us to see, not to walk within.

Long after the experiences we've had, our memories arise by triggers – which is another way to think of reshimu. A scent or flavor recognized from a past experience, a familiar face or a song may all be examples of the residue of our experiences in life, just as reshimu is a memory of the Limitless and the light which emanates from it.

To take a page from Paul from the Christian scriptures, reshimu is not unlike seeing "through a glass darkly" (I Corinthians 13: 12). It's just another clever way to invite humanity to reconciliation, reminding us that the Divine is near and available.

In our final chapter, we'll talk about Tikkun Olam and what it means in terms of Kabbalah.

Chapter Five:

Tikkun

> *"There's a crack in everything - - that's how the light gets in."*
> **Leonard Cohen**

The concept of tikkun olam (repair of Cre-ation) is one of the Lurianic Kabbalah's most potent propositions. By packaging reconciliation with a spiritual event (Shevirot ha-Kelim), Luria echoes the theology of traditional Judaism, which provides a spiritual model which today is called on and deployed in all sectors of the Faith.

The 613 mitzvot (blessed actions) are the key to Luria's tikkun. By following these commandments, practitioners restore the Holy Light of the Limit-less, wresting it from the clutches of brokenness and adding it, spark by holy spark, to the Ohr Ein Sof to be recovered by millions of others doing the same.

In Isaac Luria's historical context – the Spanish Expulsion and the resulting Jewish diaspora – the Kabbalistic explanation for the presence of brokenness and evil in the world answered a question on contemporary Jewish minds – where is God while all this is going on? That's a question many human minds ask every day. But it's the wrong question when it comes to Luria's Breaking of the Vessels.

The right question is, "what can we do about this brokenness"? Instead of asking what God can do for us, Luria's theology asks what we can do for God.

The answer is in the performance of mitzvot and applying an ethical framework to everything in life, from saying "thank you" to returning phone calls, to not walking off with a smirk when a cashier hands us more change than we're due.

This is about much more than being a "good person" or even a "good Jew." Tikkun is about being the image of God in which we were created (Genesis 1: 26-27). And what is that image?

The sefirot tell us what God looks like. We have no pictures of God because God's image is spiritual, not physical. This is the rationale behind the Jewish prohibitions against sacred imagery shared by Muslims.

When we create an image of God, we project onto Divinity our own prejudices about what God is, and that projection can be seen in the insistence that God is male – made so by centuries of male sages writing about God. Classical projection, unfortunately, did not spare Scripture. But writing creates images, and so, it might well be argued that the depiction of God as male is idolatrous.

And idolatry is what got that first set of tablets smashed by Moses (Exodus 32:19).

So, made in the spiritual image of God, we begin to understand what's expected of us. But if we genuinely understand the urgent nature of the required reconciliation, we take it to heart and begin to grow into the project of tikkun olam.

Healing

The Talmud, as we've read earlier, teaches that the broken heart is the most whole of all. In its brokenness are the potential and the herald of healing.

Just as the Shevirot ha-Kelim prefigured tikkun, it stands with it in the tension now so familiar to us in so much of Kabbalah's canon, echoing and expanding on that expressed in Hebrew Scripture and traditional commentaries.

Brokenness, as the dearly departed bard, Leonard Cohen, so poignantly points out in the quotation at the start of this chapter, is what allows the light to penetrate. In that penetration – the sudden introduction of the eternal into the material – is where the healing is initiated.

And so, in the brokenness of the Breaking of the Vessels, we encounter the nascent healing of tikkun.

Healing is a process, implicating our bodily systems in a holistic way. Our physical resources are directed toward the goal of wholeness. Our mind is focused on it. In this truth about the healing of human beings, we find the truth about the true nature of Luria's tikkun.

Tikkun is both the desired state and action that moves towards it. The act of keeping a mitzvot or modeling ethical integrity involves actions of the heart, mind, and body in union, which is its most natural state.

This corporeal analogy extends throughout the Kabbalistic idea of tikkun, as the effort is that of a whole body of people working toward the goal of tikkun olam. The reclamation, reformation, and repair of Creation result in a long-term goal – Olam Haba (the World to Come).

(NB: While this volume doesn't cover more advanced aspects of the Kabbalistic framework, you'll be interested to note that the Adam of the Garden has a mystical twin in the figure of Adam Kadmon, whose body, in Kabbalah, bears the 10 sefirot. This superimposition of the Etz Chaim on the figure of Spiritual Adam provides a template of the human body which aligns with the sefirot. See the resources section at the end of this book for more information to point you to a better understanding of this aspect of Kabbalah.)

In tikkun and the Kabbalah, which advances the cosmological model of Isaac Luria, is the promise of healing – not only the Creation in which we find ourselves but in ourselves. In apprehending a Divine purpose to our lives, broken as they are, we discover the promised "balm in Gilead" (Jeremiah 8:22), the spiritual unguent that repairs our own brokenness, freeing us to reach for the bigger picture of universal healing.

Tikkun in Wider Judaism

In today's Jewish world, the idea of tikkun olam is a familiar one. One will, in fact, find references to the idea in modern Christian literature, sermons, and discussion groups – especially in mainstream denominations.

But within traditional Judaism, the concept of tikkun was first publicly embraced and expounded upon by Shlomo Bardin (1898 – 1976). Bardin, a highly accomplished oleh (a Jew who had come to the Holy land in fulfillment of God's promises to Abraham, Isaac, and Jacob, the Patriarchs). He is remembered as a pioneer in the early years of the new nation of Israel.

In 1939, Bardin was in the United States when World War II began. He became an American citizen and founded a summer program for leadership training, following the model of the Israeli kibbutz (communal farm) system. Centered in Bardin's program was the primacy of the Sabbath.

His belief in the state of Israel as a homeland for world Jewry (the meaning of Zionism) was as "the spiritual center of one's mind." He is remembered all over the world as a revolutionary influence in Jewish education and spirituality. His work in these inter-connected fields resulted in a growing interest in the idea of tikkun and its origins in Lurianic Kabbalah.

Perhaps what's most interesting about Bardin's massively important work in the context of Kab-balah is his early entry into the establishment of young, modern Israel and his experience of the Zi-onist Youth Movement. Clearly, Bardin's interpre-tation of the meaning of Israel was closely aligned with that of the Jewish Mystics. Centering that spir-ituality in his material relationship to Israel became a growing theme in wider Judaism, outside its nor-mal settings in Jewish Mystical communities. And in his spirituality was one of the key ingredients of tikkun – action that moves the people closer to tik-kun olam and thus, to Olam Haba.

Modern interpretations, both in Judaism and in other Faiths interested in tikkun, focus on works based on creating a more just, equitable world, as well as political action. But these objectives were not the intended message of Isaac Luria's tikkun, rooted in the restoration of the peaceful, ordered Creation intended by the Creator. This was Bardin's message – that spiritual considerations take precedence to creaturely concerns.

Not that there's anything wrong with making the world a better place! But Isaac Luria had bigger fish to fry – namely, the restoration of the stewarding creature's relationship to God.

Because Olam Haba is the World to Come; the World the Messiah's return announces and brings to final fruition, the project is spiritual. It is not our version of justice. It is the Divine's, and for Luria, that demands a universal groundswell of communal action in the mitzvot and the righteousness that comes from a constant focus on God's presence, embodied in the mitzvot. This communal practice, a primary element of the reformation of a Creation longing for healing, is of a prayer prayed by the righteous every day of their lives.

Tikkun olam is unity of purpose toward a distinct goal, practiced by those dedicated to repairing the relationship between God and humanity. And while good deeds and righteous actions outside this set of parentheses qualify as mitzvot, they are not commandments, while the 613 are, indeed.

Tikkun, then, is a long-term partnership with a Creator seeking remediation of plans into which a monkey wrench had been thrown. Humanity's prayers join with the Creator's desire for a perfected Creation, making way for the Messiah and the World to Come.

Conclusion

T hank you for joining me for this brief introduction to Kabbalah. I hope I've been able to
provide you with the kind of information you can
learn from and build on as you continue your exploration of the Kabbalah and Jewish Mysticism.

I have no doubt you're far from done with the
subject. Kabbalah and Jewish Mysticism are not
the kind of subjects most are ready to take a cur-
sory glance at once they've cracked their first book.
Rather, they draw you in, inviting you to discover
a spiritual world guided by the brilliant application
of philosophical and religious teachings and concepts toward a truth that inspires.

The journey is one, I hope, you'll continue to
seek out as you learn more about this fascinating
corner of spirituality which has become increasing-
ly prominent and sought after as time has passed.
No matter what your religious background is, there

is spiritual nourishment to be had in the study of Kabbalah, and there is an inspiration to be found in the works of the sages and scribes whose lives were dedicated to producing its canon.

I encourage you to seek them out and to get to know them through the vast body of literature produced by them throughout the ages.

Again, thank you so much for reading! I wish you well on your journey and leave you with the Aaronic blessing (Numbers 6: 24-26).

"The LORD bless you and keep you;

The LORD make (his) face to shine upon you, and be gracious to you;

The LORD lift up his countenance upon you and give you peace."

References

Metzger, B.M., Murphy, R.E., 1991, The New Oxford Annotated Bible, New Revised Standard Version, New York, NY, Oxford University Press

Dan, J, 1987, Gershom Scholem and the Mystical Dimension of Jewish History, New York, NY, New York University Press, Sourced online

Dubov, Nissin Dovid, n.d., TzimTzum, sourced online at Chabad.org

Ben Shimon ha Levi, Z., 1994, Adam and the Kabbalistic Tree, Maine, USA, Red Wheel Weiser, Sourced online (Concerning the figure of Adam Kadmon).

Encyclopedia Judaica, 2008, the Gale Group sourced online at Jewish Virtual Library

Mualem, Shlomy, 2002, What can be Shown Cannot be Said: Wittgenstein's Doctrine of Showing and Borges's 'The Aleph'", Pennsylvania, USA, Varaciones Borges, Borges Center, University of Pittsburg

Feldman, Menachem, n.d., Heaven and Earth, sourced online at Chabad.org

Robinson, G., n.d., Isaac Luria and Kabbalah in Safed, sourced online at My Jewish Learning

Schwartz, O., 2019, Natural Language Processing Dates Back to Kabbalist Mystics, sourced online at IEEE Spectrum

Made in the USA
Monee, IL
25 August 2024